A little duck

Rigby®

A Harcourt Achieve Imprint

www.Rigby.com
1-800-531-5015

Lily is at the farm.

"Where are the ducks?"

said Lily.

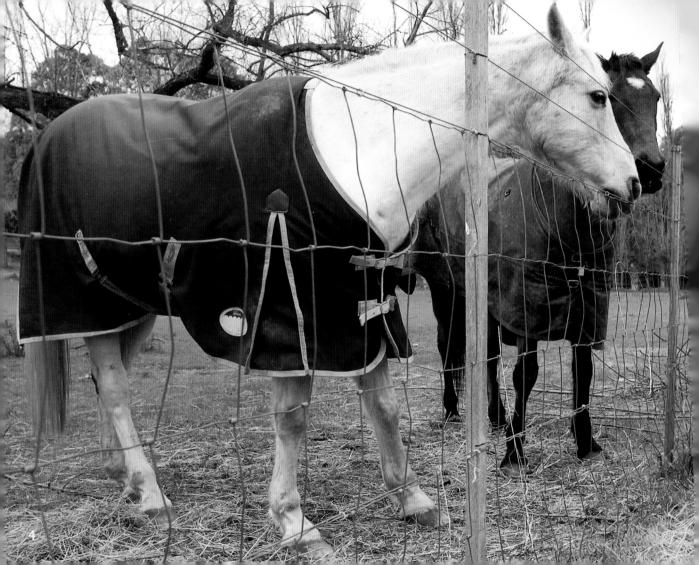

The horses are here.

The cows are here.

The sheep are here.

Here are the cats.

Here are the chickens.

Here are the ducks.

Here is a little duck for Lily.